Simple Sourdough

Also by Mark Shepard

How to Love Your Flute: A Guide to Flutes and Flute Playing
Simple Flutes: A Guide to Flute Making and Playing
Gandhi Today: A Report on Mahatma Gandhi's Successors
Mahatma Gandhi and His Myths
The Community of the Ark

*S*imple
*S*ourdough

How to Bake the
Best Bread in the World

Mark Shepard

Simple Productions
Friday Harbor, Washington

Bread loaf sketch by Lillian.

ISBN 978-0-938497-30-1

Library of Congress subject headings:
Cookery (Sourdough)
Baking
Bread

This booklet was first published by Simple Productions,
Arcata, California, 1990.

Version 1.4

This booklet tells how to make the best bread in the world. If you don't believe me, try it! No matter how much of this bread I've eaten, I've never grown tired of it.

What's amazing is that it's made from wheat, water, and salt. That's all!

I first learned to love this bread while visiting the Community of the Ark, a utopian society founded in France by an Italian disciple of Mahatma Gandhi. On my return home, a friend taught me how to make the same bread—or pretty close. Some further experimenting ended up with the method in this booklet. If you've made other breads, you'll find it refreshingly simple.

THE STARTER

Forget fancy starter recipes—especially ones telling you to add baker's yeast! Just put a little whole wheat flour in a small dish and mix in some water till it's like pancake batter. Then cover it and set in a warm place, but out of direct sunlight.

Exact amounts really don't matter, but if you need a guideline, try half a cup of flour with an equal amount of water. After evaporation, that should yield about half a cup of starter.

The starter mixture is meant to feed and fuel growth of wild "yeast"—actually a blend of various species of yeast and bacteria. Some of this yeast is in the air—especially if you're working somewhere you've already made sourdough—while some is in the flour itself.

Within a few hours to a few days, the mixture should bubble and smell sour. If the mixture crusts over before that, just stir it up. If it picks up the wrong microorganisms and smells foul, throw it out and try again.

Some flour may give you a harder time making the starter because processing may have killed or removed the wild yeast. Your best bet may be stone-ground flour, because it stays coolest during milling. You can also try flour from different whole or refined grains. Some people say whole rye is the best source of all for wild yeast.

Don't use water straight from the tap! Public water contains enough chlorine to weaken or even kill the wild yeast already in your starter mixture. While an established starter might not be seriously affected, your beginning mixture is more vulnerable.

Any bottled water should be fine. Home filtering might or might not remove enough chlorine, depending on the filter. You can also just leave tap water in an open container for two days or so to let the chlorine escape into the air. It won't do that, though, if your water utility uses the kinds of chlorine called *chloramines*.

Some environments too can cause trouble. Electric heat may reduce the number of organisms in the air by keeping it dry. Winter days with electric heat going strong and all windows closed might not offer your best chance of success.

If you get really desperate, you can always buy some starter! You should only have to do it one time.

Once the mixture bubbles, put your starter in a loosely covered jar or crock—no metal—and refrigerate it. Don't worry about "feeding the starter" to keep it fresh. Left alone, it will stay good for at least two months. When you're ready to use it, just pour off any black liquid that has formed on top—it's a harmless byproduct of the yeast.

THE INGREDIENTS

Why bother making just one loaf? This recipe makes four two-pound loaves! If that's too much for you, give the extras to friends. But watch out: They'll beg for more! (Or if you *really* don't want that much, just reduce the recipe amounts proportionally.)

You need 6 pounds—about 16 cups—of whole wheat flour. The kind to use for this recipe is flour from *hard winter wheat*. Soft winter wheat is for pastry, not bread. Hard *spring* wheat is preferred by commercial bakers and in breadmaking machines, because it rises higher and faster—but it has much less flavor. Besides, faster rising allows you less leeway in timing.

You might also like to experiment with hard *white* wheat, a newer strain that combines higher, faster rising with good flavor. (The older strains of hard wheat are red.)

Of course, if you can mill your own wheat, so much the better. Two-thirds to three-quarters cup of wheat berries gives you one cup of flour. I buy wheat berries in bulk, then run them through an electric mill.*

The only other ingredients are water and salt!

---

* In 2014, my mill of choice is the Nutrimill, which I find quieter and more convenient than other impact mills. If you're getting a slow grinder like the Retsel, I recommend steel grinding burrs rather than stones, which may deposit grit that wears down tooth enamel.

THE SPONGE

The basic method of breadmaking I use is called the "sponge method." With this, you first use half the flour to make a liquidy "sponge." Later, you add more flour to make the dough. Starting with a sponge helps develop the sourness and gluten.

To make the sponge, put 8 cups of flour in a large bowl and add all the starter you made. Then mix in warm water and beat the mixture till it's like pancake batter. Again, there's no need to be exact, but you can try an amount of water equal to the flour. You want the water warm enough that the sponge ends up lukewarm. Too cold will keep the "yeast" from multiplying. Too hot will kill them.

Now cover the bowl with a towel and leave it for a few hours or overnight.

If you don't want to use warm water, you can instead put the covered bowl where it will *get* warm—in an oven with a pilot light, or in direct sunlight, or in front of a heating vent, or on a heating pad.

You can tell your sponge is ready when it's slightly domed, smells sour, and is stringy when you stir it. If you leave the sponge *too* long, the "yeast" will eat the gluten strands, and the sponge will be runny. Your bread will wind up more sour, but it will also be heavier.

THE TWO THINGS YOU MUST ALWAYS REMEMBER

Before you make your sponge into dough, ALWAYS remember to do these two things, *in this order:*

1. Take out a small amount of sponge to be starter for your next batch. (I take about half a cup, but it could be more or less.)

2. Add salt to your sponge—2 tablespoons for this recipe of four loaves.

I won't tell you how many times I've forgotten one or the other!

THE DOUGH

To make the dough, stir most of the remaining flour into the sponge, a cup or so at a time. Stop when you can stick your fingers a little ways into the dough and pull them back clean. This is just enough flour so the dough won't stick to the breadboard. The less flour you add, the lighter your bread.

By the way, this is where you can vary the recipe. The sponge should be entirely wheat, because that's where the gluten comes from—but for the dough, you can add anything you want. For instance, make sourdough rye bread just by replacing half or more of the remaining wheat flour with rye flour plus caraway seeds.

Anything other than wheat, though, will make your bread heavier—and a bit less simple.

Here's the part you already know, if you've ever made bread. Empty the dough onto a floured breadboard and knead it till it's springy, while turning and folding it over each time. This develops the gluten and helps create pockets for the yeast to inflate. Then form the dough into four loaves and place them in oiled or greased bread pans.

THE RISING

Why not keep things simple? One rising is really enough.

For the rising, cover the pans with a towel and put them in a warm place—an oven with a pilot light, or in direct sunlight, or in front of a heating vent, or on a heating pad. The rising takes three to four hours, and there's lots of leeway.

Here's a quicker, more certain method: Turn your oven on low when you start making the dough. When your loaves are in the pans, turn the oven *off*, put the pans inside, and cover them. With this method, rising takes under two hours. REMEMBER TO TURN OFF THE OVEN!

With hard winter wheat, the dough will rise only to about half again its original height. To keep the tops from collapsing flat during baking, catch the loaves *before* they reach their maximum height. How do you tell? Listen to the crackling of the bread as it rises. When the crackling lessens, the loaves are ready.

But don't worry. You could let the loaves rise for a day or more, and they'd still turn out well enough.

THE BAKING

To get more of a final spurt to the rise, start from a cold oven, putting in your loaf *before* turning the oven on. Set the oven to 375 degrees and bake the bread about 55 minutes. You're finished when the center of the loaf reaches 195 to 205 degrees. If you take out the bread and find it's not there yet, just stick it back in for more baking.

The bread is ready to eat as soon as it leaves the oven, though it won't firm up till it cools. If you slice into it while still warm, stand it on end on a hard surface to hold in the moisture.

This bread may not need to be wrapped or bagged at all before eating, but at least wait till it's room temperature. Trapping too much moisture will soften the crust. Also, *don't* refrigerate this bread, because that dries it out quickly.

I don't know why, but this bread takes quite some time to go bad. I've travelled with loaves in a suitcase that were still good after three weeks!

FINAL FACTS

• Sourdough was the only risen bread till the mid-1800s. Baker's yeast was developed at that time—not to improve the quality of bread, but to streamline commercial baking.

• Some researchers say sourdough is healthier than bread made with baker's yeast, because the sourdough organisms break down elements in the wheat that are harmful or that lock up nutrients.

• Sourdough is easier to digest because—like yogurt—it's partially "pre-digested." Even people normally allergic to wheat can sometimes eat this bread. (To make it even easier to digest, you can toast it.)

• Whole-grain sourdough of this kind has been baked again commercially in the United States since the 1980s, most often by smaller companies. But it may not be called sourdough—look for terms like "wild yeast" and "natural leavening."

ABOUT THE AUTHOR

Mark Shepard is the author of several books on simple living and other alternatives. He can be found on the Web at **www.markshep.com**.

Made in the USA
Charleston, SC
26 September 2014